The Miracle of Meditation
A Gradual Opening Into Unbroken Trust

BY JEFF CARREIRA

The Miracle of Meditation
A Gradual Opening Into Unbroken Trust
By Jeff Carreira

Second edition
Copyright © 2013/2020
Emergence Education & Jeff Carreira

ISBN-13: 978-1-7346284-2-5

Emergence Education Press
P.O. Box 63767, Philadelphia, PA 19147

www.EmergenceEducation.com

Cover and interior design by Silvia Rodrigues

The Miracle of Meditation

A Gradual Opening Into Unbroken Trust

BY JEFF CARREIRA

My appreciation to Silvia Rodrigues
for her beautiful and truly inspired design of this book.

Introduction

These excerpts were taken from a written journal I kept during a two-month long meditation retreat. On that retreat I was following meditation instructions that asked me simply to sit still, be relaxed and let everything be as it is.

During a magical sixty-day period, I was blessed with a cascade of spiritual breakthroughs and energetic openings beyond my wildest dreams. I offer them to you to serve as inspiration for your own search for the miraculous.

. . .

It's been eight years since I wrote the words above for the first edition of this book, and nearly twenty years since the retreat that the excerpts you are about to read came from.

Reading back through this book all these years later is a wonderful experience for me. I've been teaching meditation and awakening for over fifteen years, and I can honestly say that the core and essence of everything I teach can be found in this book.

Sure, the insights here appear in an early form, seeds of ideas that I have refined and developed over the ensuing years, but still, they are here. Those two months of retreat were the most fruitful months of my life. They left me with insights, experiences and realizations that set my life on its current course.

It is a joy to read through these excerpts again and a pleasure to make them available in this new edition to serve as inspiration for your own search for the miraculous.

25
24 One Month Long Retreat Starts Tomorrow
. . . . bl.

Day 1

After only three hours of sleep, meditation this morning was difficult, but still it was obvious that if I make enough effort, I will be awake. If I am not staying awake, I am not making enough effort. *Simple.*

Each meditation today was more powerful than the last, and at times I found myself immersed in depths of stillness. I can feel the possibility of letting go radically right at hand – letting go in a way that is out of control. That is my goal, *to let go for real, to let go for good, to let go once and for all.*

I will give everything I've got to the practice of meditation and see what happens. It's wonderful that meditation is so deep, so fast, but I don't want to be satisfied with just a pleasant experience. I want to make sure something happens – something really happens.

Day 2

We did our afternoon meditation in the forest today. I wasn't expecting it to be very good. I feared it would be uncomfortable, hot and buggy. But in fact, during the first hour I felt a sense of numbness tingling in my arm. I had a moment to choose either to do something with this feeling or not. I remember thinking that I would let it overtake me, and then the numbness spread through my chest, into the rest of my body, and as it filled my head, I felt a deep relaxation descend on me. The rest of the afternoon and right up to this moment, I feel profoundly at ease. Sitting in meditation following the instructions to *"let everything be as it is"* is so easy. It is obvious that I can't help but let everything be as it is. You can't very well let everything be as it *isn't*, because that would be the way it is anyway.

In this experience of deep ease, I find that the very same thoughts that were coming and going yesterday are still here, but now I am deeply unattached to them. I am not fooled into believing they make any difference.

What is the relationship between making effort and letting everything be as it is?

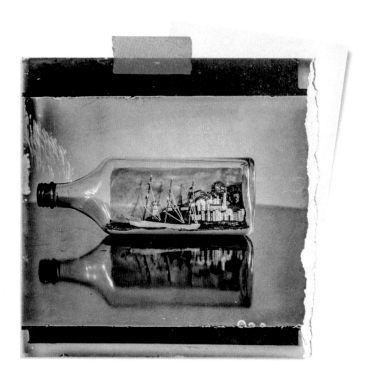

Day 3

How much time in meditation do I spend actually doing the practice — not just having more and more subtle insights about the practice, or thinking about doing it, but *actually doing it*? This morning for an instant I seemed to glimpse the possibility of what it would mean to *really* let everything be as it is. In that instant, tears flooded into my eyes, and a bolt of energy ran through me. I realized that in some deep part of my being there was a bottom-line insistence that I would never touch reality directly. That I would never let everything be as it is.

I wonder when I decided that I must always experience reality indirectly through the ever-more complex images of the mind? Even today, when meditation was so still that it felt like sitting at the bottom of the ocean, I still think there was a veil of mind shielding me from the direct touch of reality.

This afternoon my mind came at me with a barrage of thoughts and feelings, leading me to the edge of despair. I gave more than everything to following the meditation instructions, and during the last hour of meditation I found that all that had gone on earlier was destroyed; I was once again resting in stillness. Not that the thoughts and feelings went away, but I was no longer bothered by their existence.

This kind of experience fills me with the confidence that I can really go as far as I want to.

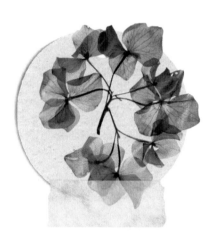

Day 4

Meditation is simply resisting the temptation to move away from where you already are.

I am so clever at finding ways to convince myself that there is a problem and that I have to go somewhere else to solve it. Once I realize that even this is not a problem, I discover that I was never trapped to begin with.

Stay with the meditation instructions.

Don't create a problem.

Just do the practice.

Meditation continues to deepen in more and more miraculous ways... Today I recognized that meditation can occur without there being any idea of "me" to support it. Being still, being relaxed, and paying attention can all happen without any idea of "one doing it all" to support it. In this I feel the possibility for radical detachment and freedom

Day 5

Meditation continues to deepen in more and more miraculous ways. Today I realized that meditation can occur without any idea of "me" to support it. Being still, being relaxed, and paying attention can all happen without any idea of "me doing it all." In this I feel the possibility of a truly radical freedom.

Today I experimented with the possibility of being able to do the practice while even letting go of the effort I was making to do the practice. It felt like meditating on autopilot. I was making the same effort, but I was resisting the temptation to be concerned about the process of doing it, just making the effort because it needed to be done. It felt like letting the effort make itself without me needing to be there.

Through the sustained practice of resisting the temptation to respond to thought and feeling in meditation, I am beginning to see clearly how much I usually respond almost exclusively to my thoughts and feelings, and nearly not at all to the objective truth beyond what I might be thinking or feeling in any particular moment. It's so easy to be profoundly unreal in this way.

Real Heart — Real Surrender

Two Insights after meditation:

1. I think I know everything.

2. I leave very little room inside myself for what I don't know.

Day 6

There is no obstacle, the only thing I could possibly be struggling with in meditation is myself. There is nothing else and no one else to struggle against. My experience in meditation is completely volitional.

I go as far as I choose to go. The content of thought is irrelevant. Whether I think a beautiful thought or an ugly one, once it is gone, it is gone. It leaves no trace. It only remains in consciousness if I make the effort to remember it. Only then does it have any lingering psychological or emotional effect, otherwise once it's gone, it's gone; as if it never happened. Thought is not real. If my attention is fixated solely on thought, then my attention is fixated solely on that which is unreal.

A knowing deeper than thought must shift in order for real change to occur. Insight alone won't change anything.

Day 7

Thoughts, they are all the same, thoughts about my life, sexual thoughts, daydreams, spiritual thoughts, all my ideas about how I am doing on the spiritual path...

...they are all thoughts, thoughts, and nothing but thoughts. Meanwhile, here in reality, I am going to die lost in my mind with all my cherished thoughts, unless I find a way out beyond my compulsive fascination with them, and the unquestioned belief that there is something in them, somewhere, of value. Just do the practice.

Stop worrying about what's supposed to happen, what is happening, what is about to happen, and what is not happening. All that thinking is just garbage, garbage, and more garbage.

In relationship to letting everything be as it is the mind produces nothing but garbage.

The last meditation tonight was deeply still. I just stopped. I didn't think about stopping, I didn't try to stop, I wasn't lost in the process of stopping; I just stopped, sat still, relaxed, and paid attention. I just let everything be as it is. So where is the explosion? Is there supposed to be one?

It became clear to me that in order to really let go in meditation, you have to intend to go all the way now—not in the future—in this moment. Only that intention can create real miracles.

Am I ready to go all the way now; am I ready to trust and surrender?

3 PASSIVITY IS DEATH

I've gotten so used to being passive I hardly notice it. I'm waiting for everything to happen to me — how about giving to the position? What about views? What about giving everything now always so that something WILL happen and you can be liberated completely from sorrow?

What about the revolution — is the revolution going to take off if I am passive? NO! What about the revolution?!

PASSIVITY IS THE ENEMY.
   PASSIVITY IS EGO
      PASSIVITY IS WAITING TO DIE

Day 8

Insight from meditation:

Passivity is death.

I've become so used to being passive in life that I hardly notice it. I'm almost always waiting for things to happen to me. What about my own commitment to making something happen? Will anything ever happen if I'm passive about it? Passivity is the enemy. Passivity is waiting.

When I really make effort to follow the instructions something starts to happen. Depth appears out of nowhere and the heavy sleepiness disappears.

Why not be free, *why not?*

Day 9

Doing the practice, really doing it with all of my attention and all of my intention, is the only thing that works. The possibility of enlightenment only exists when I am actually practicing. It will never come from trying to practice.

The mind cannot relate to this. The mind is always trying to figure out how to get enlightened and that always keeps me separate from the goal. Anything the mind thinks about enlightenment will be, by definition,

wrong, wrong, wrong, wrong...

...not true, without exception, guaranteed. Enlightenment cannot be known. The mind can't know enlightenment. All of my interpretations about the path and all my interpretations of the meditation instructions are *wrong, wrong, wrong*. The instructions are totally simple and crystal clear.

Sit still.

Be as relaxed as possible.

Be as alert as possible.

If you find yourself lost in thought, just come back to the instructions— doing the practice for real, really wanting to go all the way, never stopping, no matter what joy or bliss you feel. Never allow yourself to be tempted away from giving all of your attention and all of your energy to letting everything be as it is.

That is when the practice has power.

That is when something can happen.

Only then.

Day 10

What about not knowing? What about giving up? What about having no strategies? What about being utterly and completely helpless in the face of the unknown? What about the fact that anything that I could possibly know with the mind couldn't possibly be it?

A beautiful tension exists between knowing and not knowing.

What about sitting still, paying attention, and being relaxed and not having any idea about anything else? Why waste time trying to figure everything out? That is when real depth becomes possible.

The only bigger thrill is the dawning recognition that I can find liberation here and now.

Day 11

I constantly find that I am still trying to approach the unknowable with the mind. I seem to never give up faith in my mind even though I know it can never take me to where God is. I feel like a fool sometimes.

How does one leave the mind behind forever?

How do I let go of the mind completely?

I waste so much time and effort trying to figure out how to do it. How to know the unknowable? What folly, what useless effort. I know exactly what to do—simply be still, be relaxed, and be alert.

There is only one way to let go... by letting go.

What could be simpler?

At times in meditation it becomes blindingly obvious that nothing that I am doing or ever could do - could ever bring me any nearer to the Unknown. In those moments I feel overwhelmed by the awesome nature of the mystery and moved to tears by the knowledge that I could never touch it with the mind because it is unknowable. I think I am moved because of the pristine immaculate state of the Unknown that can never be touched by the mind and my own recognition that that is also what I am does under the veneer of mind.

Day 12

It never stops. I continually use thought and feeling to judge how close I think I am to whatever or wherever it is I think I'm supposed to be getting to.

At times in meditation it becomes blindingly obvious that nothing I am doing or ever could do will ever bring me any nearer to the unknown. In those moments I feel overwhelmed by the awesome nature of that which is truly and eternally mysterious, and I am moved to tears by the knowledge that I could never touch it with my mind. It is and will always be unknowable.

I am moved deeply by the pristine and immaculate state of that which can never be approached by the mind and by my own recognition that beneath the veneer of mind, *I am that.*

Day 13

The unbearable subtlety of how I unendingly identify with thought is overwhelming. Gross-minded thoughts are easy to recognize as only thought, but the more subtle commentary and coaching that I appear to give myself as I meditate is sometimes impossible to differentiate from who I am. I wonder if I've ever truly seen beyond the mind.

How do I reach the unknowable if not with the mind? Is there really any place to get to? Or is that an idea? Is that idea itself a problem?

As I contemplate these questions sincerely and seriously, they reveal an intense power to focus the mind. *The way to leave the mind behind is by letting everything be as it is and by assuming no relationship to thought.*

That is the way; it's just damn hard to do.

Doing practice is simply moving and liberating.

It is the student's responsibility to destroy all doubt

IT IS THE STUDENT'S
RESPONSIBILITY TO DESTROY
ALL DOUBT

URGENCY! WHERE IS THE
URGENCY! DO YOU WANT TO
BE FREE - HERE AND NOW?!?

All volition happens in the
unknown — no thought ever volitionally
did anything.
    Where does volition come from — I
don't know.
    How do actions happen — who already
them. I do — but not with thought
it happens in the unknown — somewhere
beyond thought.

I t is the
    student's
responsibility
        to destroy
all doubt.

        How do you do this?

By making the right choices
    over and over again.
By never failing to make the right
    choices.

Day 14

Limitation only exists in the mind. Only my complete identification with thought and feeling creates any sense of limitation. Outside of thought and feeling there is no limitation. Outside of thought and feeling, limitation doesn't exist. Where else could limitation exist except in the mind?

I think I know everything about how to become enlightened. At times I'm repulsed by the sheer volume of conclusions that I have about every aspect of my experience in relationship to the possibility of being free. There isn't a thought or a feeling that goes by that doesn't immediately generate a host of conclusions about that thought or feeling, conclusions about those conclusions, and conclusions about the fact that I am drawing conclusions.

I think I know everything about everything, and it is becoming painfully clear that none of it has anything to do with the truth. It is all motivated by wanting to be the knower.

Do I want to be free here and now? It is my responsibility to destroy all doubt!

How do I do this?

1. By making the right choices over and over again.

2. By never failing to make the right choices.

Day 15

All the drama, all the sincere struggle to do the right thing in spite of the obstacles, it is all a game. It is just shadow boxing because in reality there is nothing to fight against and there are no obstacles.

Beyond all my thoughts there is just me making choices and I always make exactly the choices that I want to.

Here I am between meditations, thinking that I should be more "in" than I am after two hours. How do I know where I should be? And who says that I can judge where I am at in the first place? Why not just give everything to the practice and not worry about how I'm doing?

Just let everything be as it is over and over again.

Let absolutely everything be as it is.

Once I start to let go, I see how much I don't want to give up my endless fascination with the content of my own mind.

To let everything be as it is, all you have to do is renounce the temptation not to let everything be as it is.

Who is it that is "judging the progress of my meditation" anyway? Is it... perhaps... th ego? Oh so you want to get free — let me help you with that."

"Letting everything be as it is is a totally "volitional" act. You _do_ it. Yes do it, quickly, you do it decisively and when you recognize a thought pulling you away you chop its legs out and you don't look back to see what it contained. All thought is distraction from not-knowing — All thought is temptation to doubt th Unknown. Leave it behind, and don't look back — "Let the ~~dead~~ dead bury their own dead."

I use to spend time highting off thoughts like day-dreams, fantasies, and memories. But these are the ego's crudest tools. He also has planning — but again that is crude — the most devious and subtle tools are all of thoughts that are disguised as smart and potentially valuable instruction, coachings

Day 16

Who is it that is judging the progress of my meditation?

Letting everything be as it is, is a totally volitional act.

You do it. You do it quickly. You do it decisively.

And when you recognize that a thought is pulling you away, you let it go, and you don't look back to see what it was. All thought is a distraction from not knowing. All thought is temptation to doubt the unknown. Leave it behind and don't look back.

At the start of each meditation I spend a lot of time fighting off daydreams and fantasies and memories, but these are the crudest obstacles. I am also tempted into planning this and that, but again these are crude decoys. The most devious and subtle thoughts are the ones disguised as sincere and potentially valuable instruction and coaching to myself about my practice—the "helpful" voice.

It is all just thought and by definition thought can never be the unknown.

Day 17

Often in meditation while I am struggling to let everything be as it is, I realize that nothing could ever stop me. The only reason I get distracted and start trying to change something is because a thought captivates me. But the thought didn't reach out and grab me, it just appeared, and I reached out for it. *I grabbed it.* The habit of reaching out for thought is so strong, it seems as if they grab me, but the fact is... *they don't.*

Once you move away from a thought or a feeling, really move away, really take your attention off of it without peeking behind you—once that happens—it is literally as if the thought was never there.

You pick up right where you left off in a space of no time and no thought—just letting everything be as it is. You can go as far and as deep as you want to in this. *Nothing can stop you.*

There is no limitation to meditation. You can go all the way to enlightenment if you want.

Day 18

If I think of meditation as flying an airplane and thoughts as clouds in the sky, then most of the time when I meditate, I am hoping to fly in blue cloudless skies.

Whenever I find myself beginning to fly into a cloud I veer off into clearer skies. When I am not paying attention closely enough, I can suddenly realize that I am lost in the middle of a cloud (a thought) and I can't remember how I got there.

I immediately veer off hoping to pop out into clear skies again so that I can keep flying.

I have spent hours of meditation just trying to avoid thoughts as they arise and straining to be attentive enough to remain in thoughtless awareness when I can.

How is veering my attention, every time a thought arises, letting everything be as it is?

I see how all of my mental moving around—pulling out of this thought, avoiding that one—is based on the assumption that if I am "lost" in thought then I am not meditating. If being lost in thought is the way things actually are, then how could letting everything be as it is mean trying to do something to change that?

I am discovering the possibility of flying in a straight line no matter how many clouds I go through. If I find myself in the middle of a thought and I have no idea how I got there I just don't do anything.

Practicing meditation like this means just sitting and doing nothing.

Watching as I go in and out of thought, getting lost or not, drawing no conclusions about anything at all.

More and more I am discovering the part of me that never gets lost in thought, never has, and never will. It is always awake—and in a sense always meditating.

It is the part of me I return to every time I come back from being "lost" in thought.

Day 19

The part of me that wants an experience is frustrated, even though I feel closer to the truth and more excited about the practice than I ever have. Each day in the depths of meditation my understanding of who I am and what I am doing grows more and more.

A quotation that I once heard keeps coming to me: *"The voice inside you, the one that says, 'I am going to do it, I can do it.' That's the ego. Find the place in you that is already paying attention, that doesn't have to do anything to be awake and free and stay there."*

Letting everything be as it is, couldn't possibly require any effort.

What if I really didn't have a problem?

Day 20

Yesterday afternoon, for less than an instant while sitting between meditation periods, I experienced myself as being pure consciousness. In that moment I knew that there was only one consciousness and that it was aware through every human being. I looked at the person sitting across from me, realizing that the consciousness looking through my eyes at him was the very same consciousness looking through his eyes at me.

I realized that we as human beings so deeply and constantly personalize all of our experience that we end up convinced that our consciousness is somehow separate from the one consciousness.

We believe that we are an individual mind with an individual body, living a single lifetime.

Ultimately there is only one of us.

It makes perfect sense that many spiritual masters have claimed that if you liberate yourself, you literally liberate the whole human race.

It was never the individual who was going to be liberated to begin with. It was only ever about the liberation of that one consciousness.

I'm left feeling disoriented. I still feel like Jeff, but I know that I'm not really who I always thought I was. I'm not sure what to say about that except that *reality is much, much, much, bigger than I ever realized.*

What does this mean about who Jeff is? Is he really just a collection of memories associated with a particular body? What holds it all together? What is this consciousness that falsely assumes it is a separate entity located in a particular body?

Day 21

Even the slimmest realization of Truth calls everything else into question. The only appropriate response to even a momentary recognition of "reality" is to give everything to the practice and disappear forever.

The truth of enlightenment is revealed over and over again in the experience of meditation. The highest most sublime realizations, along with the illusions of limitation, all come to light.

More and more I feel compelled to leave it all behind and rest in that awareness that was never attached to any of it.

Day 22

Meditation is becoming so deep and so still that even the desire to disappear is subsiding and I find myself in the experience of knowing there couldn't possibly be anything wrong with any of my experience because everything already is as it is.

I have lost all desire to make any discriminations whatsoever between any parts of my experience – so much in fact, that when I meditate with my eyes open, I don't even bother to focus my vision. The scene in front of me is a blur and sometimes it takes ten minutes after meditation for my eyes to readjust to being able to focus again.

My willingness not to struggle is rooted in my growing certainty that I know nothing and that I can trust in the truth of the meditation instructions.

It is so beautiful and so precious to sit in meditation. Meditation is not a means to an end. It is an end in itself. "Letting everything be as it is" is the end. What else could there be to do? Any idea I have of any place that I want meditation to take me to only stands in the way of letting go.

Where the practice will take me to is not up to me.

You must enter meditation with an unburdened mind. Keeping your mind unburdened is your job.

Day 23

The powerful experiences seem to be subsiding in meditation and I have a sense of falling more and more deeply inside myself into layers of previously unconscious volition and choice. I see that it is only the grossest most superficial layers of choice that I usually recognize to be my choices. In truth, these choices sit on a mountain of other choices. Each more superficial layer of choice is inherently limited by the choices made below. By the time you get to the obvious choices on the surface, they are so narrowly limited by deeper choices that there is almost no choice left at all. No wonder we all feel so suffocated and victimized.

What is more amazing is that all of these choices occur simultaneously, right now. *Whether I am aware of them or not, I am making choices at every level of my being, every second.* I am not limited by the choices I have made in the past. I am limited by deep and unconscious choices that I am making now in every moment.

I find it challenging at the start of every meditation to let everything be as it is. As soon as I try my heart beats faster and I feel a panic in my body. Sometimes I never move beyond this, but other times, if I am vigilant, the panic subsides, and I am overtaken by an awareness that is natural and effortless. In fact, once it starts it feels difficult to move away from and impossible to stop.

Day 24

In meditation today, I experienced the pain of "wanting" more deeply than ever before. Every desire felt painful because each one was tempting me to take my eyes off of wanting nothing. After I had sat for a long time tormented by desire, it all vanished, and in an instant, I was left peaceful and empty. No special feeling, no special insight, nothing.

I have never experienced the tyrannical nature of my need to know as I am experiencing it now. It is the strongest and most insidious form of wanting.

Sometimes it is so subtle that it is virtually undetectable. More and more I am aware of the constant activity of trying to know everything.

Trying, at times desperately, to know what everything means about me. I am hypnotically attached to it and at the same time completely tormented by it. In the deepest silence of meditation, all of my attempts to know freedom are recognized to be useless.

The mind's abstract representations of the unknowable could only ever serve to delude and confuse. I see how many of the ideas that I have held on to are just destructive nonsense when it comes to not-knowing. None of it matters in the eyes of God. It all just makes it more difficult to accept the truth when it is shown to you.

ed discrimination about your practice. The ego's "helpful" voice. — All just thought out by definition not the entrance.

The Mystery = Your Master

The Mystery = Nothing / enough
= The Absolute = Want nothing
or GURU = Everything as it is
attention always fixed on the mystery

Self-grandisement

eyes never look back and must have been chopped

Obedience to the guru

sword chops out anything that would tempt us away from the mystery

practice / renunciation
— The finder approaches naked
stripped of all — pride, arrogance,
self-importance, and any
fixed or doubted
ideas of self

Confusion

Joy

Doubt

Bliss

Insight

Fear

Adored / understanding

Judgement

Fantasy

legs keep working to the mystery

Innocent thoughts

the Finder walks on a razor sharp digital rope — the path winding through the parts of the

Despair

Memory

Desire

Day-dream

Day 25

It astounds me that I seem to have to rediscover everything everyday as if for the first time. At the end of each day, the only thing that makes my heart sing is the recognition that I know absolutely nothing about the mystery. Yet, every morning, I seem to have to wrestle all over again with the same ideas, all the same misinterpretations of the simple instructions. I seem to follow all the same dead ends, every day. Even when I can see my footsteps clearly from the day before, I sometimes feel powerless to resist retracing the same useless steps.

Eventually, I find the strength to bear the insecurity of giving up control and surrendering to the instructions once again. I sink into a place where you could never do anything but let everything be as it is, and from there *I know that all the useless meandering never really happened.*

There's beginning to be a part of me that knows the useless meandering for what it is, even when it is happening. So at least I experience less fear, doubt, and loss of intention while I am in the middle of it.

Day 26

I woke up in the middle of the night last night with a shooting pain at the base of my spine. It felt as if someone had hit me with a hammer. I tossed and turned but there was no way to alleviate the pain and fall back to sleep and so I got out of bed. I paced the room, holding my back, wondering what had happened.

At some point the pressure started building, and then a burst of energy shot up through my spine. It felt as if I was attached to a fire hose. But it wasn't water rushing through me—it was blazing white light. As the light shot up through the top of my head the brightness hurt my eyes. I tried to close them, but it didn't matter, the light was just as bright with my eyes open or closed.

After a few seconds it ended, and the pain at the base of my spine was gone. I sat on my bed and remembered things I had read about the experience of rising kundalini. I hadn't really believed them before, but now I was humbled by the recognition that they had been true all along.

What does this experience mean? I don't know.

One thing is for sure, *whatever ideas I had about what is and is not possible were rendered meaningless.* I have no idea what may happen in the weeks to come.

Ok so maybe even some of it is
true — BUT — you got yourself so
hed up in what you think you
know — and then trying to make
your own adjustments to the meditation
practice — that you ended up having to
suffer through nearly 2 hours of
meditation this afternoon just to be
able to follow the instructions and
let everything be as it is.

Your compulsive attachment to your
own stupid knowing is so strong that
you had better not take anything
for granted — YOU FOLLOW THOSE
INSTRUCTIONS UNTIL THE DAY
YOU DIE — SPIRITUALLY (ego death)
or PHYSICAL — WHICH EVER
COMES FIRST.

Things do not happen in
my way on my time — they
happen in Gods way on his
time line — Have faith in his —
trust in teachings — be patient — and
have a huge HUGE HUGE heart.

Day 27

The paradox of knowing and not knowing is endless. I am continually making my own adjustments to the meditation practice based on everything I think I know. I end up suffering through hours of meditation before recognizing that I haven't even started to follow the simple instructions of letting everything be as it is.

Letting everything be as it is requires a kind of radical trust that is beyond anything I ever imagined. When you let everything be as it is, everything—your thoughts, your thoughts about your thoughts, your conclusions about those, and the recognition that you are concluding—and on and on and on and on and on; then you start back-pedaling out of your mind, and you begin to realize that you are never going to come up against a thought that is anything more than just another thought. There is nothing real in there. My compulsive attachment to my own knowing is so strong.

Just follow the instruction.

Things do not happen in my way on my time, they happen in God's way on His or Her time. *Trust in life, trust the truth, be patient, and have a huge, huge heart.*

Day 28

Fear and doubt and pain every morning

So little faith left over from the day before

But enough

Enough faith to keep going

Knowing

There is no other way

And when the doors of perception open again

Nothing will ever have happened.

Day 29

I am seeing distinctly the voice in my mind that has always been with me—the one that I think of as me talking to myself. The one that tells me what is true and then analyzes and judges everything.

Am I speaking to myself, or is that just a voice in my head?

It amazes me how every night the meditation is stronger and more profound, but somehow by morning I most often find myself locked in brutal combat with my mind.

This morning after struggling "to follow the instructions perfectly" for a long time I became completely exhausted from all the effort. I eased back and relaxed for a minute and I realized something miraculous. I realized that I was perfectly content and that I always was. That doing nothing at all revealed perfect contentment. Tears again started to flow from my eyes and I realized that what you are pointing toward is so utterly simple and so subtle.

IF YOU TRULY LET EVERYTHING BE AS IT IS THERE COULDN'T POSSIBLY BE ANYTHING TO FEAR

Day 30

This morning, after struggling to follow the instructions perfectly for a long time, I became completely exhausted from all the effort. I eased back and relaxed for a minute and I realized something miraculous. I realized that I was perfectly content and perfectly at peace and that I always have been. Doing nothing at all reveals perfect contentment. Tears started to flow from my eyes, and I realized that what enlightenment is pointing towards is unbearably simple, subtle, and immediate.

If you truly let everything be as it is there couldn't possibly be anything to fear.

To be free, I have to be willing to be perfectly content and perfectly at peace with the person I already am. In a world as miserable as this, taking full responsibility for finding myself to be perfectly content and perfectly at peace is a big deal.

kicked out and I am naturally alert with my eyes wide open looking at the glorious splendor that surrounds me.

Periodically I am invited and carried to a pew closer to the alter so that I can see more clearly. These moments are always wonderous events. I imagine that sometime I will be carried right up to the alter where I will kneel down before it, lay my head to the ground and quietly die.

Every hour ~~I bring~~ of meditation I bring less and less fear, less and less doubt, ~~less and less~~ fewer and fewer ideas - and more and more trust, more and more confidence, more and more interest.

Sitting in meditation is like kneeling on the stairs in front of the doors to God's church, waiting to be invited in. Sometimes a whole hour goes by and the door never opens. During these times there is an almost overwhelming temptation to do ~~something~~ —To ~~pro~~ draw attention to myself, to prove myself worthy, or worse to walk up the steps, open the doors a crack and sneak myself in. But even if I manage to get in this way it isn't the ~~same~~ I can never fully relax because I know ~~that~~ I wasn't invited and ~~and~~ am always afraid that I ~~am~~ will be

Day 31

Sitting in meditation is like kneeling on the stairs in front of the door to God's church, waiting to be invited in. Sometimes an entire hour goes by and the door never opens. During these times there is an almost overwhelming temptation to do something, to draw attention to myself, to try to prove myself worthy; or, worse, to walk up the steps, open the door a crack, and sneak myself in.

Even if I manage to get in this way, it isn't the same. I can never fully relax, because I know I wasn't invited in, and I am always afraid that I will be kicked out. If I wait patiently, eventually the door opens. I am invited in and carried to a pew in the back of the church. I am perfectly relaxed because I know I've been invited in, and I can't be kicked out. I am naturally alert with my eyes wide open, looking at the glorious splendor all around me.

Periodically, I am invited and carried to a pew closer to the altar so that I can see more clearly. These moments are always wondrous events. I imagine that eventually I will be carried right up to the altar . . . where I will kneel down before it, lay my head to the ground, and quietly disappear.

Day 32

Let the instructions meditate for you.

No need to fear.

Everything will be as it is.

It couldn't be any other way.

The universe bows in gratitude to be liberated from the dream of separation.

LET THE INSTRUCTIONS MEDITATE
FOR YOU
NO NEED TO FEAR
EVERYTHING WILL BE AS IT IS
IT COULDN'T BE ANY OTHER WAY

Day 33

I sit down in meditation intent on following the instructions to let everything be as it is. I become more and more still, and then I notice all the subtle movements happening in my mind almost behind the scene—taking attention off this thought, removing attention from that feeling, putting attention here or there, very subtle, almost imperceptible, continually trying to control the show.

Sometimes I'll just stop and relax, and things will sink more deeply, but more and more often I catch myself and I feel something jump out of me that says, "Wait a minute, you're not supposed to do anything, not even stop yourself from doing something. *You're supposed* to let everything be as it is—and that must include all of your attempts to control everything."

And then I feel an outrageous confidence that seems to taunt my mind. "Go ahead," it says, "do anything you like, move your attention all over the place for all I care, think and feel whatever you want, no rules, anything goes."

At that point there is a moment of insecurity and I am certain that this is definitely not the right thing to do. After a few minutes, I have an experience that I can only describe as falling asleep while you're still awake. I feel a deep relaxation descend over me and my body becomes partially paralyzed. I have deeply surrendered and given up all control.

I realize that there is nothing to do, because I know that I am going to let everything be as it is, and so no matter what I do, everything is still going to be as it is.

Things will start out as they are, I'll do whatever I think I am doing, things will end up exactly as they are, nothing will ever have happened, nothing has ever happened, nothing could ever happen; because there is only one thing and that one thing is everything, and it always is as it is.

There is perfect rest and contentment and that is all. There really is no problem in this world.

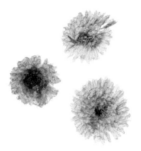

Day 34

At one point in meditation tonight I was so tired that my eyes were watering, my head was aching, my muscles were stiff, and my mind felt as thick as mud. But I was determined that I was not going to fall asleep. Then a thought went through my head that said, "You're not actually tired." And *I realized it was true*. At that instant something very powerful happened in my awareness. I still had exactly the same sensations, but I realized that all I was doing was looking at the inside of an incredibly tired body. I realized that if I had slept for ten hours and had just woken up, and was completely refreshed and opened the curtains to a bright sunny morning, the awareness that was seeing that sunny morning would not be any more awake than the awareness that was looking at the inside of my tired body. I realized that awareness is always one hundred percent on and that I am never any more or less aware than that. There is no way to turn awareness down.

When I actually did go to sleep later, I laid down on my back and closed my eyes and felt a numbness starting at my feet and moving up my legs engulfing me like a cocoon. I felt a mild vibration and realized that I had fallen asleep, but I hadn't lost consciousness. I thought, "Oh, my God, I'm asleep." I fell deeper into sleep. My breathing became rhythmic and I realized that I couldn't move. Eventually, I lost all sensation of my body and was aware only of blackness.

In the middle of this blackness a scene emerged in front of my eyes. It was a gas station and I was on my back with four huge men each holding one of my arms or legs, and they were pulling me apart. Around them was a ring of other men who were chanting, "You've got to go." I quickly realized I was dreaming and that my mind had activated, obliterating the blackness. When the mind was asleep, I was in blackness and when the mind woke up, it was as if someone had turned on a light and a dream erupted. Then, just as suddenly as the scene had appeared, it disappeared again, and I returned to the blackness. That went on through the night until the morning when the alarm went off and I felt my body wake up. I thought, "Now I'm awake, whatever that means."

There was no difference between sleeping and waking. I was the continuous thread of awareness that had watched the process of falling asleep, was aware throughout the night, and had woken up in the morning. In the morning I thought, "This is exactly what's going to happen when I die. It will be one continuous stream. I will have a body, then the body will fall away, and I will return to the blackness of pure consciousness."

Day 35

The meditation never stops!

Like a river that always flows beyond the mind, the meditation is always there. I lie down to go to sleep at night and I am meditating deeply. I wake up from sleep and I am still meditating. I haven't gone anywhere. I meditate when I eat, I meditate when I sit, I meditate when I walk.

The meditation never stops!

Day 36

I cannot believe that after doing this much meditation for this long, it is still endlessly, endlessly, endlessly, illuminating in ever-new ways.

The state of being aware and identified only with consciousness itself allows me to see the mind and all of its objects and mechanisms as things that exist outside of me.

It is endlessly illuminating and thrilling.

Day 37

There is a depth in meditation becoming available to me that is overwhelming, not just going deeper than ever before, but discovering a whole new realm of depth.

I taste oblivion in meditation and recognize it to be my own true self. I believe the experience of oblivion is the experience of consciousness when it is completely unattached from mind.

I want to experience myself fully.

I want to know the truth.

You are Truth

Your nature is Oblivion

Day 38

If every illusion of a personal and separate existence was completely eradicated from the universe, can you imagine what consciousness would create then?

Can you imagine?

...if consciousness itself had absolutely free and unimpeded control over every individual human form?

It is profoundly humbling to realize that liberation is actually liberating and to see what a know-it-all I have been in the face of the Truth.

I am beginning to experience what it means to disappear into oblivion, and it is igniting my passion for true freedom. All that matters is that the joy that has been given to me can inspire others to trust.

Then on no short cuts in Meditation!!!
You have to let anything be as it is – You have
to only slowly to the bottom
The bottom has certain characteristics
but you can't remember those and try to
recreate them later – You just can't

Day 39

There are two things that I find continually amazing!

1. My experience of the human condition never changes one single bit, even after nearly six weeks of intense practice. Some part of me always wants me to think that it is different, but it isn't.

2. From the liberated perspective, seeing the human condition in action is utterly captivating and unendingly fascinating.

There are no shortcuts to meditation. You have to let everything be as it is. You have to fall slowly to the bottom. The bottom has certain characteristics, but you can't remember those and try to recreate them later, you just can't. If you try, you torture yourself.

You have to let everything be as it is—*everything*—no matter how wrong you think it is. Even if you find that you are not letting everything be as it is, you still have to let that be as it is, too.

Somewhere, of course, you were the whole time, how could you not be?

Day 40

It literally feels as if something is available in the universe that wasn't before. My experience in meditation is that I am overtaken by eternity.

To call it infinite vastness would give form to the formless.

It can't be known, described, or even experienced and yet it is there. I find myself captivated by a spontaneous ongoing contemplation of the unknown and the boundless vastness of existence.

Day 41

Every time I taste the non-dual, I cry because I know I'm home.

There is no separation. Find it. Point to it. You can't.

There is only that. Everything appears from the unknown. Thought comes from the unknown; the inspiration for thought comes from the unknown and so on and so on. And yet, here I am, appearing as the one who is seeing thoughts and making decisions.

I am beginning to accept that I will never understand what I have been trying so hard to know.

Day 42

Any trace of doubt in the face of the absolute could only ever be insistence on knowing the unknowable.

Everything is falling together in the most unexpectedly simple and miraculous way. In meditation today I recognized that I was looking for something. Not a totally defined something, but some particular experience. When I let go of that, I am just sitting. Thoughts come, capture my attention for a while, and go. Feelings do the same. Sometimes there is no thought or feeling and I am consciously aware of making effort to follow the meditation instructions.

Even though thought and feeling seem to be shifting and moving, I never stray. Even if I seem to get lost in thought I never move. It's hard to imagine that anything could be so simple. There is no wanting for anything to be other than it is—just simple contentment and peace. No fireworks, no tremendous insights, just peace.

This must be the kind of relief that most people only experience at physical death.

Day 43

The more you sit and let everything be as it is, the more you realize

there's nothing to do. Anything I think I'm doing to somehow let everything be as it is, couldn't be. It would have to be some variation of trying to change things. It's agonizing because it means giving up all control. I can't liberate myself. I can only look and see the truth and let it be as it is.

The more I sit, the more I see that there is only the awareness of what is. There's nothing else, no duality, no separation, no me.

Separation is only caused by the sense of "I," which in the end is only an unending stream of thoughts that say, look what I'm seeing now, look what I'm thinking now. Look, those are my thoughts. Look at what I'm doing now. I should be doing this, etcetera, etcetera.

There's no separate "I."

I feel so delightfully confused.

Where are the words coming from that this hand seems to be writing?

Day 44

I don't want to pretend to know anything; I only want to say what my experience is.

Some things are becoming clear, others I do not understand. But I trust that all things will come in time...or not. You literally let everything be as it is, no matter how much your experience seems to be wrong and you seem to be doing the wrong thing; *you just let it be exactly what it is.*

Day 45

Meditation tonight was fascinating. I was letting everything be as it is, I was deeply peaceful and quiet, and I started to observe some very simple and subtle movements of my mind and body. I saw how a thought arose and led to a feeling that led to relaxation in the body, or a sharpening of attention.

I was just observing, and at some point, I had the overwhelming sense that something was moving me. I knew I was not the originator of the movements, and I had the unmistakable sense that something was trying to figure itself out through me, in me.

I feel deeply unhinged. These experiences come and they are so powerful, they literally fill my eyes with tears, but I have no idea what to make of them at all. I can see how easily I could claim everything for myself simply by adding an ongoing commentary of, this is me, here I am, I am here too, and this is also me, etcetera, etcetera.

21st Century Shria

Having no identity does not mean that suddenly "I" will not know who "I" am — it means not any concept of Jeff and his history will be erased completely out of the universe.

It will not be replaced with a new identity, with God or anything else "no identity" means "no identity", not "having no identity"

Day 46

It is a deeply sobering thing to even begin to recognize what true freedom really is, and even more sobering to realize that I really do want to disappear to who I have been. Deeply, deeply, deeply, I want the pure awareness that I have discovered to be free from any sense of me.

It is profoundly sobering and miraculously glorious all at once.

I really do want to be free.

Having no identity does not mean that suddenly I will not know who I am. It means that any concept of Jeff and his history will vanish from the universe, it will not be replaced with a new identity, with God, or anything else, no *identity* means *no* identity; not me without an identity.

When I was very young I would lock myself in the bathroom and stare into my own eyes in the mirror and wait for some magical moment that would make my body expand until it was as big as the Universe.

THE NEED TO KNOW
COULD ONLY EVER
BE DOUBT IN THE
ABSOLUTE!

Reckless Indifference to the Future!

live with
RECKLESS INDIFFERENCE
to the
FUTURE

Day 47

Meditation is becoming so still. I don't have any desire for anything. I feel absolute indifference. I don't care about the world. I don't even want enlightenment. I don't care about myself or anything that I ever was. The only thing left is an ineffable yet strong feeling of love and the desire for the end.

The need to know could only ever be doubt of the mystery!

Live with reckless indifference to the future.

I sat in meditation tonight for an entire hour identified only with being the awareness of what is. Jeff's fictitious history of neurosis is yielding to the overwhelming reality of oneness. Not knowing is the key to everything because I know I will never understand what is being revealed. There is only this moment. *I am this moment.*

I once heard thoughts described as abstract representations of historical events. The "event" is the very instance that knowing emerges in the mind. The moment after knowing emerges, a thought wraps around it, but it's too late, the event has already happened.

I have been hunting for an imagined place called oblivion. But oblivion is always here. Time and space are an illusion generated by thought. In reality there is only one dimension. It is an infinitely small dot of eternity.

Day 48

When I was very small, I used to look at myself in the bathroom mirror and stare into my eyes. I would make a particular effort, which I know now was the effort of letting everything be as it is. Eventually, the back of my head would open up to eternity and I would know that I was as big as the universe. I did this often; because I was compelled by the experience and because I wanted to check to be sure that the vastness was still there. One day, it wasn't there anymore.

When I was a little older, I started locking myself in my father's car, closing my eyes, and trying to force my mind to stop thinking. Eventually, I realized that was impossible, so I started watching how one thought led to another. I was very carefully looking for a gap between thoughts that was big enough to squeeze through. I never found one.

Still later, on warm summer nights, I would lie in the grass for hours, staring at the stars, overwhelmed by the immensity of the cosmos; but it was too late. By then, I was completely convinced of separation.

Eventually, I gave up, and went to the mind looking for answers. The fictional history of Jeff was all that remained.

Now I am home again, the back of my head is completely blown open to the eternity that I am.

No words can ever express enough gratitude.

Meditation was so beautiful tonight. I was way out beyond the mind and the fire of Enlightenment was like a blazing steam going through me. I wanted so badly to merge with that steam and I was making effort to let go into it forever. Then I realized that my desire to merge with IT was IT and the effort I was making was IT. I relaxed so deeply and fell to a depth that I have never felt before.

There is no need to worry.

EVERYTHING is literally taking care of itself.

TRUST and go.

Surrender is the acknowledgment, realization, and acceptance of that which is beyond understanding.

The only thing to do in meditation is to let everything be as it is. because it is over!

Any attempt to do anything is a denial that the end has come.

Renunciation is refusing to respond to that which is unreal.

Meditation was so beautiful tonight. I was way out beyond the mind and the fire of enlightenment was like a blazing stream going through me. I wanted so badly to merge with that stream and let go into it forever. Then I realized that my desire to merge with it, was it, and the effort I was making was also it. I relaxed and fell into a depth that I have never felt before.

There is no need to worry.

Everything is literally taking care of itself.

Trust and go.

Surrender is the acknowledgement, realization and acceptance of that which is beyond understanding.

The only thing to do in meditation is to let everything be as it is, because it is already over. Any effort to do anything is only doubt that the end has come.

Day 50

There is no one meditating, there is only the explosion of life, the fire raging, everything is that fire. My desire to merge is that fire, my effort to merge is that fire and even all of my false ideas of self are that fire.

There has only ever been one, no matter how it seemed. I never wanted to be free, there was never any me to want such a thing.

It always wanted to be itself and I thought it was me wanting to be free.

Day 51

It is over. Becoming for Jeff is ended.

He is not enlightened. The tendency to personalize, to create the apparent reality of the separate individual remains, but that does not matter. Jeff is dead; he is unreal, even if the tendency to believe in him continues.

I can't believe how just letting everything be as it is can continually bring you to more and more depth even after all these weeks of retreat.

I want to go all the way to the bottom.

When I have no memory there is no me.

Day 52

The human race is headed toward a final convergence, and the final convergence that I am currently experiencing in myself is that very same convergence.

Although there has always been a more obvious stream in the flow of my life, there has also always been this alternate unbroken line leading right to this final convergence. This alternate line has been continuous through all of human history. The eyes of the entire race will eventually turn away from separation and become transfixed by the mystery of who we are.

At the impact of final convergence, the human race will finally discover what it truly is. I don't have any idea how long this will take, but it will happen.

Day 53

Enlightenment is the profoundly humbling recognition and acceptance of the fact that there has always been something more important than "me" happening.

Day 54

Letting go and not knowing

Letting go and not knowing

Trust and surrender

Trust and surrender.

Meditation is so powerful. Tonight, when meditation began, I thought to do absolutely nothing at all. For a few seconds I experienced myself only as free-floating awareness, and then the meditation became very deep, very quickly.

At some point I thought, "I'm going to let everything go, even the idea of letting everything go," and then I came to a dead stop. Not that I had really been moving anyway, but the sense of motion that I now realize is always with me, stopped, completely.

I was just sitting in the room as if I had slipped out of time. At one point I began to feel a strong pressure building up on my skull and face and after a while I began to hear a high-pitched buzzing sound. The buzzing grew until it was a column of energy shooting out of the top of my head and I felt like I was being sucked out of myself as if through a straw.

In the middle of it, I just relaxed and let it be as it is. The combination of pressure and energy repeated itself slowly a few times before the meditation ended, and again I became aware of myself as only free-floating awareness.

Later, when I was walking around outside, I realized I no longer knew where the boundaries were located. Even here, walking around in the world of limitation, I really don't know what the limits are.

There is only one false idea and that is the idea that this is all there is.

"This" refers to whatever I happen to be experiencing at any moment. When I continue to break through this one idea, I continually have no idea how much more reality there is beyond what I happen to be experiencing.

The only thing that stops me from going all the way is my belief that I have reached a limit and that going further is not possible.

I have never been hungry,

I have observed hunger arise in this body, but I am always full.

I have never been lustful,

I have observed lust arise in this body, but I am always satisfied.

I have never wanted.

I have observed desire arise in this body, but I never needed anything.

I am completely overwhelmed by everything that is happening. My mind is being totally obliterated. It keeps racing to try and create theories that will explain what it experiences in some linear fashion so that it can locate itself, but I have no idea what is happening or where I stand in it, at all. My personal sense of self is being totally overwhelmed.

Day 56

It has never been clearer to me that it has always only been me who has been holding on to the mind. Look what I have been clinging to. *Underneath all of the feelings of victimization, it has only ever been me who has been holding on.*

At one point in meditation, I decided to stop breathing and let the body naturally take over the rhythm. It worked. I was meditating, becoming very still, nodding backwards into sleep. I have felt this many times in meditation and have always reflexively snap myself back to awareness. This time I didn't – I just fell backward – FULLY AWAKE! It was like falling into a black hole or the mouth of a volcano.

I didn't try to stop it from happening. I just kept falling, slowly. Periodically, I felt an intense pressure on my face that would slowly yield, it was like falling in slow motion through the floors of a building.

I went into meditation this morning only
wanting to make absolutely no effort and
just watch what is REALLY TRUE reveal
itself. In no time I was completely swept
up with the current of liberation that kept
surging through me for the entire hour. This is
all so totally thrilling!!!!

Make absolutely NO effort!
Wowe!
Zero!

Day 57

The experience of meditation tonight was perfect undifferentiated being, there wasn't even a ripple that I could point to and say, "that's me." There was nothing but unbroken beingness and non-existence. It was like floating in the current of a slow-moving river. As long as I didn't move at all, there were no ripples, but if I moved or resisted the current even a tiny bit, I created ripples, and the ripples were the only sense of identity there was.

All I need to do is get out of the way.

Surrender means giving up control.

I can see clearly that there are two forms of pride: one is wanting to be the enlightened one; the other is wanting to be the humble one who does not own their own enlightened experience. Exactly between these two is the most torturous and beautiful place. It requires no effort to live exactly between these two.

I went into meditation this morning wanting to make absolutely no effort so that I could simply watch the truth reveal itself. In no time, I was completely swept up into a current of liberation that kept surging through me for the entire hour.

This is all so utterly thrilling

to make absolutely no effort at all

none

and to discover

zero

Its as if everything has always only been a rushing blur of ecstatic energy – but at some point I blocked all the energy from going through me so that I would be able to differentiate myself from everything else – of course I can't really block it so I really just block all awareness of it – that is what the ego does – it creates a separate sense of self by blocking all evidence to the contrary – including any sense of the rush of energy that I am and that all of life is.
UNBELIEVABLE !!!!

I do not want spiritual experiences – I want to be free, free, free, and forever always only free.

Day 58

My head is going to blow up and I can't wait.

I am being erased in ecstatically torturous successive stages of voluntary death and rebirth. The massive rush of energetic love that has always been the only thing that is happening is all that I could ever possibly be. If I look closely, I see that it has always been rushing everywhere through everything, one huge surge of energetic love. This is what I experienced as a child, but even then, I personalized it and thought it was in me.

It is as if everything, including my sense of being me, has always only been a single rushing blur of ecstatic energy. Somehow, I have blocked all awareness of this and created a separate and solid sense of self.

I do not want spiritual experience; I want to be free, free, free, and forever always only free.

Day 59

Letting everything be as it is, making no effort at all, and never moving, like Jesus in the desert or the Buddha under the Bodhi tree.

Many temptations arise, but I resist, and the karma of a self-indulgent life burns away, painfully, but without suffering, free, free, free, and forever always only free.

At the start of meditation tonight a thought ran through my mind, "To make no effort at all requires only trust." I immediately slipped into a state of deep trust where letting everything be as it is seemed totally natural. The entire hour passed in unbroken trust, even if I became lost in thought, even if I found myself making effort to do something. Trust in myself, trust in life, but the best way to describe it was simply trust, absolute, unbroken trust—the willingness to be unguarded, undefended, and open.

I have a journal filled with descriptions of outrageous experiences that occurred during this retreat, but I would gladly trade them all for this one hour of unbroken trust, one hour of being in a perfect, loving relationship with life.

Day 60

Once again, this morning I experienced deep trust, but I also recognized a sense of uncertainty about it. I could see that I wanted to see myself trusting so that I would know that I trusted.

At one point I looked at myself looking at myself and, in that instant, nothing changed, and everything washed away. I once again fell into the experience of perfect trust, which is not the experience of knowing that you trust. It is simply the experience of everything as it is.

I was exactly who I was, with all my insecurities and all my attempts to squash them, and it was all perfect, just as it was. I felt no desire for anything more, and no desire to be other than who I already was.

Enlightenment has nothing to do with becoming the person I think I need to be. It is all about being who I already am.

Being free couldn't possibly require any effort. If I am making effort, it could only be because I want something besides freedom.

Epilogue

After being back from retreat for two days I am really beginning to see just how totally different EVERYTHING is.

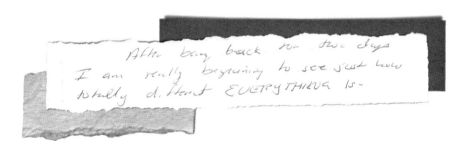

About the Author

Jeff Carreira is a meditation teacher, mystical philosopher and author who teaches to a growing number of people throughout the world. As a teacher, Jeff offers retreats and courses guiding individuals in a form of meditation he refers to as The Art of Conscious Contentment. Through this simple and effective meditation technique, Jeff has led thousands of people in the journey beyond the confines of fear and self-concern into the expansive liberated awareness that is our true home.

Ultimately, Jeff is interested in defining a new way of being in the world that will move us from our current paradigm of separation and isolation into an emerging paradigm of unity and wholeness. He is exploring some of the most revolutionary ideas and systems of thought in the domains of spirituality, consciousness, and human development. He teaches people how to question their own experience so deeply that previously held assumptions about the nature of reality fall away to create space for dramatic shifts in understanding.

Jeff is passionate about philosophy because he is passionate about the power of ideas to shape how we perceive reality and how we live together. His enthusiasm for learning is infectious, and he enjoys addressing student groups and inspiring them to develop their own powers of inquiry. He has taught students at colleges and universities throughout the world.

Jeff is the author of numerous books including: *The Art of Conscious Contentment, No Place But Home, The Gift of Spiritual Abundance, The Experience of Luminous Absorption, Embrace, Philosophy Is Not a Luxury, Radical Inclusivity, The Soul of a New Self,* and *Paradigm Shifting.*

For more about Jeff or to book him for a speaking engagement, visit: www.jeffcarreira.com

Made in the USA
Columbia, SC
28 May 2020